BACKYARD BUGS

Louise Spilsbury

Published 2011 by
A&C Black Publishers Ltd.
36 Soho Square, London, W1D 3QY

www.acblack.com

ISBN   HB 978-1-4081-3384-2
       PB 978-1-4081-3383-5

This book is produced using paper that is made from wood grown in managed, sustainable forests. It is natural, renewable and recyclable. The logging and manufacturing processes conform to the environmental regulations of the country of origin.

Produced for A&C Black by Calcium. www.calciumcreative.co.uk

Printed and bound in China by C&C Offset Printing Co.

All the internet addresses given in this book were correct at the time of going to press. The author and publishers regret any inconvenience caused if addresses have changed or sites have ceased to exist, but can accept no responsibility for any such changes.

Acknowledgements

The publishers would like to thank the following for their kind permission to reproduce their photographs:

Cover: Shutterstock
Pages: Dreamstime: Aprilleigh1352 14, Petr Malohlava 16, David Mark 11, Sergeytoronto 5; Shutterstock: Alle 20, Joseph Calev 19, Anton Chernenko 9, Cre8tive Images 18, David Good 8, Cathy Keifer 15, Jakub Kozák 10, Tanya Mass 7, Orion Mystery 13, Gherasim Rares 21t, Sapsiwai 17, Ljupco Smokovski 21b, Marek R. Swadzba 4, Wong Hock weng 12, Yellowj 6.

Contents

In Your Backyard

There are creepy crawlies all over your backyard!

Shapes and colours

Some bugs are long and thin. Others are round. Bugs come in different colours, too.

Aren't I pretty?

Eye

Feel your way

Many bugs have **antennae** on their head. They use them to feel their way around.

Antenna

Most bugs have huge eyes.

Ladybirds

Ladybirds are great climbers. They can climb up almost anything!

Don't eat me

Ladybirds taste nasty. They are red and black to warn birds not to eat them.

Ladybirds can walk upside-down.

Spot

Count my spots!

Many ladybirds have seven black spots.

Hold tight!

Centipedes

Centipedes are not fussy eaters.
They eat any bugs they catch.

See me run

Centipedes have lots of legs.
They can even run backwards.

Leg

Dinnertime

Centipedes catch food with their **claws**. They chew it in their **jaws**.

Jaw

Claw

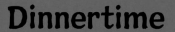

Look at all those legs!

Can't catch me!

Grasshoppers

Grasshoppers have amazingly long back legs. They use them to jump.

Listen up!

Grasshoppers also use their legs to hear things. Their ears are in their knees.

Knee

Many grasshoppers are green.

Talking legs

Grasshoppers make a noise by rubbing their legs and wings together.

Hop it!

Shield Bugs

Shield bugs are the same colour as leaves. This helps them to hide from birds that eat them.

In hiding

In spring, shield bugs are green, like the leaves they eat.

Can you see me?

Smelly shield bugs are also called stink bugs!

Changing colour

Shield bugs turn brown in autumn, like the leaves.

Shield bug

Spiders

Garden spiders have a clever way of catching small bugs to eat. They make a **web** of sticky **silk**.

Sticky spot

Flying bugs get stuck on spiders' sticky webs. Then spiders eat them.

Here comes dinner!

Fly

Snack time

Spiders sometimes wrap a fly in silk and save it to eat later.

My web is super-sticky!

Ants

Ants tell each other where food is. They leave a trail of smelly footprints from the food.

Follow that smell

Ants follow the smelly trail to the food. Then they carry it back to the nest.

Yum, yum!

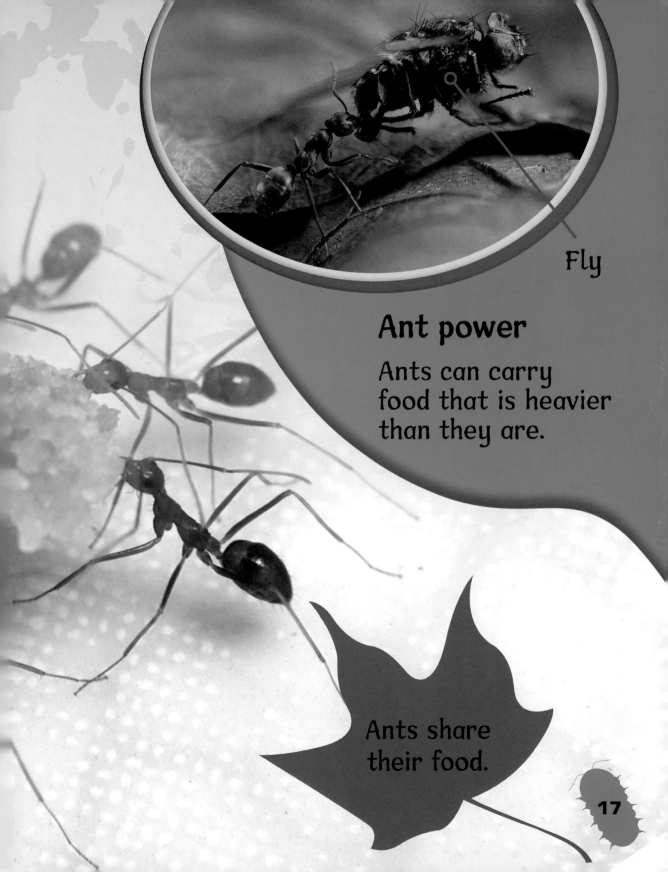

Fly

Ant power

Ants can carry food that is heavier than they are.

Ants share their food.

Woodlice

Woodlice have super-tough **shells**. Some woodlice have bendy shells, so they can curl up.

Drink up

Woodlice drink through their bottoms!

Bottom

Woodlice use antennae to feel their way.

So tough!

18

Roll up, roll up!

Some woodlice roll up into a ball if they are frightened.

Antenna

Bees

Bees have strong wings. They fly from flower to flower.

Making honey

Flowers make a sweet juice called **nectar**. Bees use it to make honey.

Bees fly a long way.

20

Storing honey

Bees store honey in cells they make inside their nest.

BZZZZ!

Glossary

antennae two long thin parts on an animal's head. Bugs use antennae to feel and smell things.

cells little spaces inside a bee's nest. Bees store honey inside these cells.

claws sharp, curved parts of an animal's body. Animals use claws for catching and holding things.

jaws mouth and sometimes teeth of an animal

nectar juice found inside a flower. Bees use nectar to make honey.

shells hard covers over some or all of an animal's body

silk fine, soft thread made by spiders. Spiders use silk to make webs.

web trap that spiders make to catch flies and other bugs. Spiders build webs from silk that they spit out.

Further Reading

Websites

This website shows you how to make a bug hotel and a bug-friendly garden to attract bugs to your garden. Find it at:
www.buglife.org.uk/discoverbugs/bugactivities

Find out how to spot bugs in your garden at:
www.nhm.ac.uk/nature-online/life/insects-spiders/bug-forum/?q=gallery

Find out more about ladybirds and other bugs and animals that might come into your backyard at:
www.rspb.org.uk/wildlife/wildlifegarden/atoz

Books

100 Things to Spot in the Garden (Usborne Spotter's Cards) by Simon Tudhope, Usborne (2009).

In the Garden (Nature Walks) by Clare Collinson, Franklin Watts (2010).

RSPB My First Book of Garden Bugs by Mike Unwin, A&C Black (2009).

Index